GREECE

Major World Nations

GREECE

Garry Lyle

CHELSEA HOUSE PUBLISHERS
Philadelphia

Chelsea House Publishers

Copyright © 2000 by Chelsea House Publishers,
a division of Main Line Book Co.
All rights reserved.
Printed in Malaysia.

First Printing.

1 3 5 7 9 8 6 4 2

Library of Congress Cataloging-in-Publication Data

Lyle, Garry.
Greece / Garry Lyle.
p. cm. — (Major world nations)
Includes index.
Summary: An overview of the history, geography, economy,
government, people, and culture of Greece.
ISBN 0-7910-5385-7 (hc.)
1. Greece—Description and travel—Juvenile literature.
[1. Greece.] I. Lyle, Garry. Let's visit Greece. II. Title.
III. Series.
DF728.L93   1999
949.5—dc21   99-19154
CIP

ACKNOWLEDGEMENTS

The Author and Publishers are grateful to the following organizations and individuals
for permission to reproduce copyright illustrations in this book:
British European Airways; The Food and Agricultural Organization of the
United Nations; Robert Glover; The Greek Embassy in London; The Reverend
J. Laughton; The National Tourist Organization of Greece.

Contents

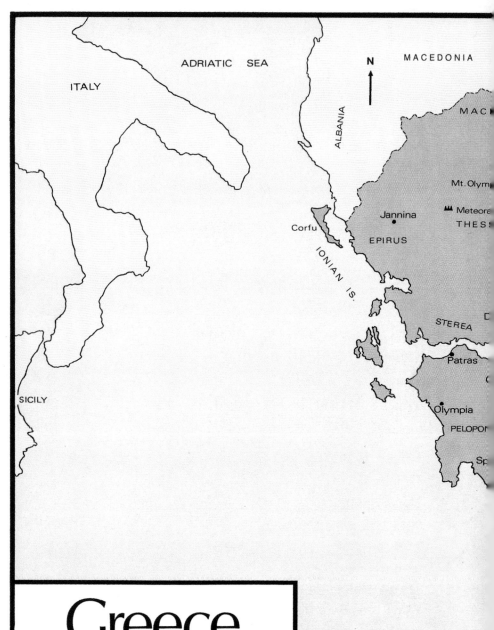

ITALY

ADRIATIC SEA

MACEDONIA

N

MAC

ALBANIA

Mt.Olym

▲▲▲ Meteor

Jannina

Corfu

EPIRUS

THES

IONIAN IS.

STEREA

Patras

Olympia

PELOPON

SICILY

Sp

M

Greece

Scale

| 0 | 25 | 50 | 75 | 100 Miles |
| 0 | 25 | 50 | 75 | 100 | Kilometres |

FACTS AT A GLANCE

Land and People

Official Name   Hellenic Republic (*Elliniki Dhimokratia*)

Location   Southern Europe between Albania and Turkey, on the Balkan Peninsula

Area   50,949 square miles (131,940 square kilometers)

Climate   temperate with mild, wet winters and hot, dry summers

Capital   Athens

Other Cities   Thessaloniki, Piraeus, Patrai, Peristerian

Population   10,541,000

Population Distribution   Urban, 65.7 percent; rural, 34.3 percent

Mountains   Pindus

Highest Point   Mount Olympus, 9,570 feet (2,917 meters)

Official Language   Greek

Religions   Greek Orthodox, 98.6 percent; Muslim, 1.5 percent

Literacy Rate	95.2 percent
Average Life Expectancy	Male, 75.6 years; female, 81.4 years

Economy

Natural Resources	Bauxite, petroleum, marble, magnesite
Division of Labor Force	Services, 52 percent; agriculture, 23 percent; industry, 25 percent
Agricultural Products	Olives, grapes, melons, peaches, tomatoes, tobacco, cotton
Other Products	Wine
Industries	Textiles, food processing, tourism, mining, petroleum
Major Imports	Machinery and transportation equipment, food, chemical products, crude petroleum
Major Exports	Textiles, food, petroleum products, cotton
Currency	Drachma

Government

Form of Government	Parliamentary republic
Government Bodies	Parliament
Formal Head of State	President
Head of Government	Prime Minister
Voting Rights	Compulsory voting for citizens 18 years of age and older

HISTORY AT A GLANCE

About 2,000 B.C. The Hellenes (Greeks) migrate from the north to the land now call Greece. Knossos and Mycenae are built.

c. 1200 B.C. The Greeks battle the Trojans and are victorious.

1200-900 B.C. The Dorians invade, conquering their cities and forcing the Greeks into slavery. This period becomes known as the Dark Age of Greece.

800-600 B.C. Called the Archaic Age. Athens becomes a more powerful city-state. Homer writes the *Iliad* and the *Odyssey*.

776 B.C. The first Olympic (Panhellenic) games are held between the city-states of Greece.

600-500 B.C. Sparta becomes a powerful city-state

490 B.C. The Persian army invades Greece and is fought off at the battle of Marathon.

480 B.C. Persia again invades Greece, this time entering the country on a bridge of boats. There are numerous battles in the Persian Wars but the Greeks eventually are victorious.

10

475-400 B.C.	The Golden Age of Greece sees Pericles come to power and Athens rises in power. The government as a democracy is organized. Some of the great philosophers of all time can be found in Greece during this time–Socrates, Plato, Aristotle, Diogenes, and Epicurus.
447 B.C.	Construction of the Parthenon is begun.
460-404 B.C.	The city-states of Athens and Sparta are at war through most of this period (the Peloponnesian Wars). These wars eventually lead to the fall of Athens as a great power and the devastation of most of the Greek city-states.
359 B.C.	Philip becomes king in the Greek state of Macedonia and sets out to unite all of Greece. Macedonia now becomes the center of power.
336 B.C.	Philip of Macedonia dies and his son, Alexander (Alexander the Great), succeeds him. Alexander leads the armies of Greece to conquer lands in Asia Minor, Egypt, Persia, and parts of India.
1st-4th centuries	Greece is now part of the Roman Empire.
324 A.D.	Emperor Constantine moves his capital from Rome to Byzantium and renames it Constantinople. Constantine brings Christianity to the whole area.
1453-1821	Greece and all the surrounding lands falls to the Turkish Empire and Greece enters its hardest and unhappiest centuries. Lands are confiscated, taxes imposed, men are forced into the Turkish army. A tax is put on church attendance, trying to deter the practice of Christianity, but the Greeks pay the tax rather than give up their religion and the churches hold the Greeks together as a nation.

11

1821-1831	The Greeks begin their fight for freedom from the Turks and become a free independent state in 1832.
mid-1800s	Independence is difficult and the Greeks cannot agree on a form of government. They eventually decide to make a foreigner, Prince Otto of Bavaria, their king, hoping that an outsider will be able to unite the many factions vying for power. It doesn't work and Otto is driven out of the country.
1914-1918	The Greeks force their king, Constantine, to enter World War I against the Germans and King Constantine leaves the country in protest. Greece, standing between Germany and her Turkish allies, helps to defeat them.
1920	The Greek army, again led by King Constantine, invades Turkey and is crushed. This disaster brings revolution at home and the government is unsettled for many years.
1936	John Metaxas tries to bring the methods of governing being used by Hitler in Germany and Mussolini in Italy to his Greek homeland.
1939-1944	At the start of World War II the Greek people refuse to go to war on the side of Germany and Italy. The Germans invade Greece leading to starvation, torture, and widespread destruction of its people and cities. The Greeks fight an "underground" war against the invaders.
1944-1949	A long civil war ensues over the type of government Greece should have. The government changes hands 17 times.

1949-1967	The country becomes a democratic kingdom and settles into rebuilding its war-torn cities and industries. It starts to prosper economically but political unrest continues.
1967	In April the military takes control of the government. Political parties are banned and many leaders are arrested.
1968	King Constantine II calls for the overthrow of the military regime and has to go into exile.
1973	The military regime holds a country-wide vote and the people choose to become a republic again, this time with a president instead of a king. A new civilian government is appointed.
1981	Greece becomes a member of the European Economic Community but the new socialist government with Andrea Papandreou as prime minister argues for withdrawal from this and NATO. Papandreou will remain prime minister for almost 15 years.
1990s	Tensions between Greece and her neighbors, Turkey, Macedonia, and Albania, mount as the political situations in those countries change.
1995	The United States and the European Union intervene in negotiations for the end to tensions between Greece and her neighbors.
1996	On January 15, a very sick Papandreou is forced to resign. He dies on June 23. Konstantino Simitis succeeds him as prime minister.

14

1

Greeks to Us

Have you ever heard someone say "It's all Greek to me"? If you have, you will know that he meant "Here's something I can't begin to understand." And a glance at the five-letter word on these postage stamps will show you why. Two of the letters are familiar enough. They look like the *E* and the *A* of our own alphabet, and they have nearly the same sounds as our *E* and *A*. But what can you make of the other three, with nothing but our own alphabet to help you? Or what can you make of all five even if you are told how to change them into letters from our own alphabet? By making the change, we get the six-letter word *HELLAS*; but that is still Greek to us—unless we know something of Greece already, and have found out that the people who live there call their country Hellas, and call themselves Hellenes.

Why do *we* not use their names? Well, the story is an old one, more than half as old as the story of Greece itself. About 2,700 years ago, the Hellenes were beginning to find that their country was not fertile enough to grow all the food that they needed, nor

15

rich enough in natural products to keep them all employed. So they started to spread overseas. You will see from the map that some were bound to try spreading into Italy, a larger, richer, emptier country only a short distance across the Adriatic Sea.

Among the first to move there were a group who called themselves *Graikoi*–that was the name of a tribe, like Clan Gregor in Scotland, or Igbo in Africa, or Judah in the Holy Land of Biblical times. They settled to the south of Rome and, because they called themselves Graikoi, the Romans began to call all Hellenes *Graikoi*. Later, they changed the spelling to Graeci and called the home country of these people Graecia. Later still, with yet another change, the names came into our own language as Greeks and Greece.

The Graikoi brought more than their tribal name from Hellas to Italy. They knew how to write, and the Romans did not. So the Romans borrowed their letters, changed the shapes and sounds of some to suit their fancy and their own Latin language, and called the result an *alphabet* after the first two Greek letters, *alpha* and *beta*. That Romanized Greek alphabet became our alphabet–which explains why the *E* and the *A* on the stamps were familiar to you even if you could not read the other letters. The settlers from Greece brought more than their alphabet, too. After the letters came words, and the ideas behind the words. For instance, if we want to be amused, many of us go to a theater to see a comedy, or if we are feeling more serious we may choose to see a tragedy. But theater and comedy and tragedy are all Greek words, and Greek ideas. The shape and equipment of our theaters and the patterns of our plays and much of our music–also a Greek word—have developed from models and methods that came to western Europe from Greece by way of Italy. Much of our art and literature, science and technology has been influenced by ideas and examples that reached us in the same way.

The Romans became great builders. Wherever their empire spread, they left roads, bridges, aqueducts, docks, temples, law courts, and huge defensive walls. But such things cannot be built without plans, and none but the simplest building work can be planned or completed unless the planners and builders have some knowledge of arithmetic and geometry, both of which are Greek words. These subjects are branches of mathematics (another Greek word). To the ancient Greeks mathematics was a study of such importance that over the entrance to the greatest of all Greek schools there was a notice meaning "Keep out if you're no good at geometry." So it will not come as a surprise to you to hear that the Romans learned their mathematics from the Greeks, and through the Romans it came to us, together with a Greek introduction to physics, chemistry, biology, surgery, geography and most other sciences.

Even now, when modern science has taken us so far from the Greek beginnings, scientists and inventors usually turn back to the old Greek language when they want to name something new. Cinema is a Greek word; television and hydrofoil are half-Greek words; photograph, helicopter and microscope are made up from Greek words—as are hundreds of other English nouns, including that very modern word astronaut, which is simply a shortened form of the Greek for "star-sailor."

Nor do we stop with science. However imperfectly they may practice it, most nations of the modern world believe in some form of democratic government—government to suit the wishes of the people, by the people themselves, or by their freely chosen representatives. And our earliest models of democratic government, like the word democracy itself, came from Greece. There can be no true democratic government without the attitude of mind that makes people want to govern themselves. If you simply accept what is there, if you do not make a habit of asking why it is there and whether it should be there, you are an easy prey for what the Greeks called tyrants—rulers who put their own needs, wishes, and benefit before those of the people they govern. And the Greeks as a whole were never easy prey for tyrants; they were, above all, a questioning people.

They believed that a human being, however humble, has a right to ask questions and receive answers, and to let his own reason sift the lies from the truth. And they applied their questioning habits not only to political life, but also to humans themselves, to their origins, their behavior, and their futures, and to the universe of which they are a part. This they called philosophy, which means the love of wisdom and knowledge, and from Greek philosophy came our first lessons in logic—the art of thinking clearly and thinking straight, of finding our way to the truth by the use of reason. The Greek philosophers also gave us many of our ideas about law, education, and citizenship; and it was they who laid the foundations of science and mathematics which in our own time are taking us out to the stars.

In their fierce respect for human dignity, for the worth and the rights of each individual as a separate and special person, the Greeks stood almost alone in the ancient world. Only in the Jews do we find a similar outlook, and an equally strong desire to know what is right and what is wrong, what is good and what is bad. So perhaps it is not surprising that when we look for the source of what is good and lasting in western civilization, most streams lead back to a mainstream in which the ideas of Jews and of Greeks come together.

But what of the Greeks themselves? What was happening to them while their ideas were shaping our world? And what kind of people were they to produce such ideas? Those are questions we should answer before we look at their country today—at the dry, rugged, sea-washed corner of southeastern Europe where over 10

A farming village. Donkeys are widely used to transport people and goods.

A Greek farmer and his wife.

million of their descendants still live, still struggle for a democratic way of life, still search for answers, and still very often find it hard to make a living.

2

Greece As It Was

Greeks say that when God was creating the world he looked at the earth, and saw that it was very stony. So he sifted it, sprinkling the clean soil far and wide; and in time the clean soil became the

"The stone-heap became Greece." Farming the rocky ground is a difficult way of making a living for many Greeks.

fertile countries. As for the stones, he let those fall in a heap and the stone heap became Greece.

There are good reasons for that story, as some of the pictures in this book will show you. But it is not wholly fair, all the same. Greece is indeed a rocky country. About two-thirds of its 51,000 square miles (132,000 square kilometers) are highlands and islands bare of anything but scrub and heath, unfit for any kind of farm work but the herding of goats. Yet about one half of its 10,540,000 people live by farming the rest. And no one who has seen the vineyards and the citrus groves of the south, the wheat-fields of the midlands, or the cotton and tobacco fields of the north could say that the rest is not fertile.

Tobacco leaves hung up to dry on a farm in the north.

Much of Greece is too bare to feed any animals but goats, and the goats help to keep it bare by nibbling new growth.

Those farming areas are mostly plains and valleys, which are warm and easy to travel through. About 4,000 years ago they began to attract settlers from the north: cattle-grazing tribesmen who spoke an early form of the Greek language, and who were the ancestors of the first Hellenes. Where their northern homeland lay, we cannot be sure. But we can make a guess at somewhere in the cooler regions, because they had fair skins and fair hair, and they were used to drinking beer made from barley, not the wine of warmer lands. We can guess too that they had lived a long way from the sea, because it appears that there was no word for "sea" in their language. They had to borrow one, the word

23

thalassa, from the language of the Pelasgians, a smaller, darker people whom they found in the central and southern parts of their new country.

The newcomers—we may call them Greeks even though this name came later—were a stronger people than the Pelasgians. Over the centuries when they were spreading through central Greece and into the Peloponnese, many Pelasgians fled to neighboring islands, and even further. Some may have traveled as far as Britain. And those who stayed among the Greeks had to accept Greek rule, to use the Greek language, and to give over their holy places to the gods of the Greeks, letting the goddesses whom they worshiped take second place. But the Greeks were intelligent as well as strong. So they were very willing to learn from the more civilized Pelasgians, who themselves had learned much from the island people of Crete.

Straddling the sea-routes between Europe, Asia, and Africa, Crete was a natural trading center and resting place for the slow, oar-driven ships which carried the sea-cargoes of those days. And the Cretans had built up a rich and powerful sea-trading empire. Much of their wealth was put into what we would call by a Greek name—technology. As planners, builders, and inventors, as craftsmen in stone, metal, wood, and cloth, they were very far in advance of the almost-primitive Greeks. But these same almost-primitive Greeks had all the abilities of the highly civilized Cretans. They had lacked only an example. And, in following the Cretan example, they became prosperous and powerful themselves, powerful enough to challenge their teachers.

A wall-painting in the ruins of Knossos, a palace of ancient Crete. Here, so the story says, Theseus killed the Minotaur.

Do you know the story of Theseus and the bull-headed Cretan monster called the Minotaur? Theseus was the son of a king of Athens, one of the many small kingdoms that had grown up in Greece as the Greeks settled in. Every year, his father had to send 14 young people to the mighty king of Crete, to face the Minotaur and be killed by its horns. And one year Theseus put himself among the 14. But Theseus was not killed. Instead, he killed the Minotaur, and led his companions back to Athens. Told like that, the adventures of Theseus are no more than a story. But much of his people's history is hidden in stories. And in this one lies the fact that there came a time when the Greeks broke the power of Crete. Perhaps they were helped by earthquakes, which we know destroyed many of Crete's magnificent buildings and weakened her people, but in any case the mastery now moved to the mainland, and the Greeks themselves began to seek wealth and power abroad.

Another familiar story, about Jason and the Argonauts, reflects the fact that voyages were made to begin trade with the primitive but rich peoples who lived around the vast Black Sea. And yet another, the famous tale of the wooden horse of Troy, comes from a struggle between the Greeks and the people of Troy for control of the narrow entrance to the Black Sea, and of the coast lands of Asia Minor.

Troy fell to the Greeks in about the year 1200 B.C., but they had little time to enjoy the results of their victory. They quarreled among themselves and, while they were quarreling, new waves of Greek-speaking peoples swept down from the north.

The invaders, called Dorians, were rougher and more warlike than the earlier Greek settlers, and were at first unwilling to accept the civilization that they found. They broke up kingdoms, destroyed cities and palaces, and stifled trade. And they turned the people who had defied Crete and conquered Troy into serfs and refugees. Many of the refugees fled across the Aegean Sea to make new settlements in Asia Minor and the Aegean Islands. Meanwhile, Greece itself moved into what some history books call the Dark Age.

The Dark Age lasted over three centuries; but dark is the right word for them only if we take it to describe a time about which we know very little. It is very much the wrong word if it makes us think that civilization kept going backwards, or even stood still. Progress there certainly was; when light falls on Greece again we find the Dorians settled and more civilized, the old Greek kingdoms dividing themselves into city-states—that is, independent states each consisting of one city and the countryside around it—and a population grown big enough to be ready for the migrations that took Greek ideas to Italy and even further west. We find too that the Greeks have their alphabet and the beginnings of their written literature in Homer's two great story-poems the *Iliad* and the *Odyssey*. And that they are about to make a nationwide event of the Olympic Games, a festival held every four years at Olympia in the Peloponnese.

Our modern Olympic Games are called a revival of the Greek games, but a Greek of ancient times would probably disagree, and not only because the modern Olympics include much that would surprise and perhaps shock him. To the ancient Greeks, the games were first of all a religious festival, held in honor of the Greek god Zeus in the grounds of his Olympian temple. Their program allowed for music, storytelling, and spoken poetry as well as athletics, because the ancient Greeks were not inclined to think of "brain or brawn" as we often do. Neither the athlete nor the artist despised the other's interest, and the ideal man to the Greek was the "whole" man, one who could "fell an ox with one hand and compose a song with the other." By the way, Zeus and the other Greek gods are sometimes called the Olympians, but the name has nothing to do with the Olympic games or the temple of Zeus at Olympia. It comes from Mount Olympus, a wild

Ancient Olympia—the athletes' training ground and the ruins of their changing rooms.

and widespread peak 200 miles (320 kilometers) northeast, near the opposite corner of Greece. Olympus, almost 10,000 feet (3,000 meters) high, is always misty, often snow-capped and sometimes violently stormy, and the Greeks believed that the home of their gods lay along its upper ridges, behind a curtain of cloud and storm.

Though rather bad-tempered and quarrelsome himself, the god Zeus was said to prefer it if the Greeks lived at peace with each other, and one great achievement of the Olympic games was that they did help to keep peace among the many rival city-states. Every Olympic year was a year of truce, a "cooling off" year when quarrels were put aside for the sake of the games, and then perhaps talked out peacefully instead of being fought out. So the

Olympics became very important politically, important enough for Greek historians to date events by them. Instead of numbering the years individually as we do, they grouped them into the four-year periods between games, and called each group an Olympiad.

Through the first 74 Olympiads—the three centuries after 776 B.C.—the Greeks were approaching their Golden Age, the age whose thought and skills and discoveries did so much to shape our own civilization. But to make Greece secure for the Golden Age they had to fight off another invader. East of the Greek colonies in Asia Minor, the great military empire of Persia was expanding towards Europe. It swallowed Asia Minor and some of

At Thermopylae, modern Greeks have built this memorial to the Spartans who defended the pass in 480 B.C.

the Aegean Islands; and, in 490 B.C., a Persian army landed in Greece, 26 miles (42 kilometers) northeast of Athens. But they came no further. A much smaller army of Greek citizen soldiers, mainly Athenians, drove them back to the sea after one fierce battle. The battle was fought on the plain of Marathon. And we call the long-distance race in the modern Olympic Games the Marathon to commemorate an Athenian athlete who killed himself running back to Athens with the news of victory.

Ten years later, Persia tried again. 400,000 Persian soldiers marched across the strait between Asia and Europe on a bridge of boats, and turned southward down the coast of Greece while 800 Persian warships sailed abreast of them. At Thermopylae 300 Spartans, descendants of the Dorians who had broken the first Greek civilization, died to a man delaying the Persian army. Off the island of Salamis, a Greek fleet led by the Athenians scattered the Persian ships. And at Plataea, northwest of Athens, Greek soldiers, with Spartans to the fore, met the Persian army again and drove it from Europe forever.

Athens and Sparta were now the strongest city-states. And unhappily they could not agree. The Golden Age that followed the Persian Wars was brought to an end by quarrels between them, quarrels that extended to the other city-states and at last cost all of them their independence. The Macedonians, their related (but much less civilized) northern neighbors, forced them to accept the rule of the Macedonian kings. And the young king Alexander, afterwards called the Great, was more concerned with winning an empire abroad than with preserving the Greek way of life at home.

He led conquering armies through Asia Minor, south into Egypt, and then eastward through Persia as far as India.

Asia and Europe came closer together and gained much from each other as a result of Alexander's conquests. But his empire scarcely outlasted his own short life. The later Macedonian kings could hold neither it nor their Greek subjects. As the Greek cities now proved too weak to stand as separate states, Greece became a province of Rome, the rising western empire that had already taken over the rich Greek colonies in Italy.

Like the British of a later age, the Romans had been greatly impressed and influenced by the thought and achievements of the Greeks and, as masters of Greece, they did much to restore its importance. Athens became a flourishing city again, the educational and cultural center of the empire; and, in 324 A.D., the Emperor Constantine began to move the political center from Rome to the old Greek city of Byzantium (in our own time called Istanbul and part of Turkey). Byzantium, rebuilt on a much grander scale and renamed Constantinople in honor of Constantine, also became one of the two main centers of the new Christian faith. From its birthplace in Judaea, Christianity had been spreading widely through the Roman Empire, taking in Greek ideas as it spread, and using the Greek language. Constantine's own mother had been a Christian. He himself stopped the persecution of Christians, and consecrated the new Byzantium as a Christian city. From the new Byzantium developed the Orthodox churches, to which most Christians in eastern Europe and western Asia now belong.

At Daphni near Athens, this mosaic picture of Christ looks down from the dome of a church built when Greece was ruled from Byzantium.

When the Roman Empire in the west collapsed, Byzantium preserved an eastern empire and Greek civilization for more than 1,000 years. But it allowed the rest of Greece to decay, and to suffer from long periods of invasion by some of the barbarian hordes who were spreading from central Europe, and later by Crusaders who proved better at helping themselves to estates in Greece than at rescuing the Holy Land from the Turks. Then, in 1453 A.D., Byzantium itself fell to the Turks, and Greece entered the hardest and unhappiest centuries of her long history.

The Turks were of the Muslim religion. With the Crusades to remember, they had little reason to think kindly of Christians. And they showed it in their treatment of the Greeks. Farmlands were confiscated, and leased back to the Greeks at crippling rents or worked at starvation wages by Greeks for Turks. Heavy taxes, including a tax for attending a Christian church, made the people poorer still. All men, and even some young boys, were forced to serve in the Turkish army, and to fight for Turkey in wars that destroyed buildings and art treasures from the distant Golden Age. Resistance to Turkish rule was punished cruelly. Only one freedom remained to the Greeks—the freedom to attend their churches so long as they paid the tax. They did pay the tax, and through nearly four centuries of Turkish oppression the churches held the Greeks together as a nation, a nation always looking to the day when it would win back its independence.

Others were looking to the day of Greek independence, too. Towards the end of the 18th century, the climate and the ancient culture of Greece began to draw visitors from western Europe. What they saw made many of them philhellenes, a Greek name meaning "lovers of Greece." There grew up a strong feeling that the Turks should not be allowed to treat the birthplace of European civilization as something very near to a slave-state.

So, many philhellenes and also their governments gave help

A procession commemorating the siege of Missolonghi in the war of independence. Many philhellenes, including the British poet Byron, died during the siege.

when, in 1821, the Greeks began a struggle to free themselves. The struggle lasted ten years, and even then the Greeks of the north and of several islands remained under Turkish rule. But the others were free to form an independent state, which they did in 1832.

3

Greece As It Is

In appearance, the Greeks who emerged from 15 centuries of Byzantine neglect and Turkish tyranny were very different from the tall, fair-skinned Hellenes who had founded their nation, or even from their much closer ancestors of the fifth century B.C., the century of the Golden Age. You can see that very clearly if you

Sculpture from the beginning of the Golden Age.

A Greek of our own century.

look at statues and vase-paintings of earlier Greeks in a Greek museum, and then make contrasts with the modern Greeks.

Tall modern Greeks there certainly are, and fair Greeks too. But in 4,000 years of mixing with darker, differently built peoples the first Hellenic type has disappeared. Most modern Greeks are dark and fairly small, with faces that rarely look like those in ancient sculpture and vase-painting. They are not wholly like the earlier Greeks in thought and behavior, either. Christianity, Turkish rule, and links with other peoples have made changes in their outlook as well as in their appearance. But they *are* descendants of the earlier Greeks. And, because the earlier Greeks had devoted so much thought and experiment to methods of government, some people

36

believed that when the Turks had gone the modern Greeks would have no political troubles.

They were very much mistaken, perhaps because they had not allowed for three ways in which modern Greeks certainly resemble their ancestors—they delight in argumentative talk, they find it hard to agree among themselves, and they are not very good at working as a team or at accepting leadership. As a result, and also because of foreign interference and because some Greeks managed to grow very rich while the rest of the people remained very poor, Greece had difficulty settling on a form of government after it won its independence from the Turks.

For a short time after the war of independence, the country was a republic. But the Greeks had split into quarreling groups even while they were fighting the Turks, and the new government could not bring them together. The first president of the republic was assassinated. Civil war seemed very likely. And then, against the wishes of many Greeks, their most powerful leaders decided that the country would be more peaceable as a kingdom with a foreigner as king. Also against the wishes of many Greeks, they chose a young German prince, Otto of Bavaria, who had no knowledge of Greece and no confidence in its people. For the first ten years of his reign, he treated the country almost as though it were a German colony, and ruled it mainly through German officers. So the Greeks began to feel that their hard-won independence was being lost again. They rebelled, and finally forced him to give up the throne.

To find a new king, the Greek leaders turned again to foreigners, and this time chose a member of the Danish royal family. As King George I, he ruled Greece for 61 years, but he too failed to please the Greeks or to settle their differences. He died by assassination, and his reign might have ended sooner but for a long and successful struggle to win back the islands and most mainland regions which the Turks had kept after the war of independence.

Shortly after King George's death, the First World War began. His son, the new king, Constantine I, favored the German cause, even though Turkey was also on Germany's side. But, by that time, the Greeks had a democratically elected parliament; and the party in power, led by the great statesman Eleftherios Venizelos, wanted Greece to join in the war on the side of Britain and her allies. Parliament had its way. King Constantine left the country, and his son Alexander became king. Greek soldiers helped to defeat Germany by standing between her and her Turkish allies.

The end of the war gave back to Greece the last of her mainland regions to have been ruled by Turkey. But it also brought her more troubles. In 1920, Prime Minister Venizelos and his party lost an election, and King Alexander died. Perhaps rashly, a majority of Greeks agreed to let King Constantine come back. Certainly rashly, the new government sent the weakened Greek army to invade Turkey, where nearly three million Greeks were living. Turkey hit back much harder than the Greek government had expected. The invading army was crushed. Many of the resident Greeks were killed; and about two million were expelled to Greece, where they had to live in great poverty and discomfort, depending mainly on foreign help because Greece itself was too poor to provide most of them with food, homes, and work to support themselves.

This Turkish disaster brought revolution at home. King Constantine lost his throne again and some of his ministers were executed. For 11 years Greece was an unsettled republic, with increasing poverty, much unemployment, and little money for relief or for the development which could have provided more work.

Meanwhile, the dictators Hitler and Mussolini had taken control of Germany and Italy, where unemployment and poverty had also caused much unrest. Their methods were brutal, but they seemed to be improving conditions a little. In 1936 a Greek, John Metaxas, tried to follow their example. After a revolution which gave Greece a king again, Metaxas persuaded the king to let him rule as a dictator. His attempt to cure unemployment was stopped by the Second World War, when Germany and Italy tried to conquer the rest of Europe. Because Metaxas had been copying Hitler and Mussolini, they expected Greece to help them. But whatever Metaxas may have wanted, the people of Greece said "No." In the Greek language, the word for "No" is *Ochi*. And among the Greeks the date on which they refused to help Italy and Germany is still celebrated as Ochi Day.

They have bitter reason to remember the first Ochi Day. It brought about four years of German occupation in which thousands of Greeks lost their lives, thousands more suffered starvation, injury, and torture, and much of the country was laid waste. Like their neighbors in the former Yugoslavia and Albania, the Greeks put up a fierce "underground" resistance to the Germans.

Also like the Yugoslavs and Albanians, many of the Greek resistance fighters came to believe in Communism. And when the occupation ended they tried to make Greece a Communist state. However, they succeeded only in throwing their country into a long civil war which wasted more lives and resources, and gave Greece 17 changes of government between 1944 and 1949.

After 1949, the country became a little more settled. As a democratic kingdom and with much help from the United States and Britain, it began the rebuilding and development which unemployment and poverty had made so necessary. Busy shipyards gave Greece the world's largest fleet of oil-tankers and its third largest merchant navy. Metal works, chemical plants and oil refineries were established. Extension of electricity supply gave country areas a chance to begin light industries. And, in Athens, a nuclear research center began to work on the peaceful uses of atomic energy. Agriculture—the country's main industry—was also developed, and new markets for fruit, tobacco, and other farm produce were found when Greece became the first associate member of the European Economic Community (now called the European Community and part of the European Union.)

But the beginning of improved living conditions did little to improve political conditions. The Greeks could still not agree among themselves. There were many conflicting political parties, and neither of the two most powerful ones could obtain a majority large enough for good government. One of them was also believed to be supporting another attempt at Communist revolution. To prevent this a group of senior army officers, with the

Men of the United Nations Food and Agricultural Organization help farmers in the dry regions of Greece by showing technicians how to seek and use underground water.

army supporting them, took control of the government in April, 1967. Political parties were banned. Some of their leaders and many suspected Communist sympathizers were arrested. A non-party national government, under the direction of the army officers, was set up. This new government began an attempt to create what it called "the conditions of security, order and equality which will make it possible to operate a parliamentary system in Greece on a sound and healthy footing."

At first the king, Constantine II, appeared to support the new government. But in 1968 he called for an attempt to overthrow it, and left the country. The attempt failed. The king had to stay in exile and, in 1973, the military rulers held a referendum in which the voters chose to make Greece a republic again, with a president instead of a king. Meanwhile, the military rulers had gained support from some of the people by reducing unemployment, improving social services, and extending a development program begun by an earlier government. They had also promised that free parliamentary elections would be held when the country seemed rather more settled. Those elections never took place, although the military rulers did appoint a civilian government after the referendum of 1973.

However, this new government lasted less than four months. Before the end of the year, military rulers had taken charge again; but they, too, lasted only a few months. They had become very unpopular because they persecuted and imprisoned people who preferred civilian government. In 1974, the Greeks returned to democracy. They also decided that they would not invite the king to return, but would keep their republic. Since then, Greece has had a democratically-elected president and parliament. But there were still political problems which made the future seem a little uncertain.

Among these problems were relations with the countries of western Europe and with the United States. After withdrawing from the North Atlantic Treaty Organization (NATO) in 1974, Greece rejoined it in 1980. And, early in 1981, Greece became a full member of the European Community. The election in 1981 voted in a socialist government and Andreas Papandreou became prime minister. Papandreou remained in office for nearly a decade but socialization of the economy and culture failed. In 1990, a new election saw Konstantinos Mitsotakis elected prime minister, followed by the reelection of Papandreou in 1993. Tensions between Greece and her surrounding neighbors increased in the

42

A village blacksmith outside his smithy. Many Greek farmers still rely on the village blacksmith for their tools and equipment.

1990s due to the changing political scene in those countries. In 1996 a very sick Papandreou was forced to resign and was succeeded by Konstantino Simitis.

This long story of struggles, wars, and changes explains why Greece did not progress very quickly after Turkish rule ended. Nevertheless, the Greeks are not an unhappy, dissatisfied people. They manage to enjoy life very much, often a great deal more than people in richer and more developed countries. And they are much too friendly and well-mannered to embarrass visitors with

43

their political troubles. In fact, it is only their very great kindness which is embarrassing. The Greek word for foreigner, *xenos*, is also the Greek word for guest; in Greece, any foreigner is treated not only as a guest, but also as an old friend. If you ask a Greek to direct you, you can take it that he is very busy indeed if he merely tells you the way. He is much more likely to see you safely on it, or even go the whole distance with you. If you happen to be in a country district he will probably insist on taking you to his home for a meal first, and on giving you a bed if the end of the day is near. However poor he may be—and many Greeks are desperately poor—he will expect nothing in return. He looks after you because he has inherited from the ancient Greeks the feeling that kindness to strangers is a duty, and because he has a very warm interest in other people. Foreigners sometimes mistake his interest for inquisitiveness, or even impertinence. He will ask you your age and how rich you are, what your grandfather did for a living and why you are wearing such clothes. But he has no intention of what we call "prying," and he would be very surprised to hear that some people think it rude to ask personal questions of strangers. To him, such questions are a part of his hospitality. He wants to know about you because he wants to know you, and he wants to know you because he thinks of you as a friend.

This feeling of friendliness to strangers does as much as the kind climate to encourage foreigners to live in Greece. Many do live there, not only as individuals, but as communities with differences of custom, religion, language, and clothing which are always respected by the Greeks.

44

Mainly in and around the city of Thessaloniki, Greece has a community of Jews whose ancestors found refuge among the Greeks when they were expelled from Spain about 500 years ago. The community lived there unharmed until it met German persecution during the Second World War. It was these Jews who began the tobacco-growing industry which is now so important to Greece.

In the mountainous regions south of Thessaloniki live the Vlachs, a shepherd people who came to Greece even earlier than the Jews, and who still live as a community with their own language, customs, and types of clothing. There are gypsies, too, and colonies of Bulgarians, Albanians, Armenians, and Slavs, all of whom found refuge and a chance to live their own way of life in Greece when it was denied them in their home countries. Even the Turks have found it possible to live comfortably and undisturbed in independent Greece. In parts of Thrace, the northeastern province, nearly half the population is Turkish. Men wear the *fez* (the red, tasseled cap of the Muslim religion) and women are veiled in the Muslim style. Some of the newspapers are printed in Turkish and some of the schools use the Turkish language. There are Muslim mosques with slim minarets instead of Christian churches with belltowers; and old Turkish houses with walled gardens and latticed windows. Sometimes there are even camels, descendants of those who brought the silk and spices and ivory of the Far East across Asia to Byzantium.

But now let us leave the north for a while, and begin our closer look at Greece in the far south.

4

Down South

Athens became the main city of ancient Greece, and it is also the capital as well as the largest city of modern Greece. But it very nearly was not the capital. The Greeks began their struggle for independence in the Peloponnese, the southern region which on the map looks a little like a gnarled human hand with the fingers pointing to the island of Crete. Much of the struggle was directed from Nauplia, a small and very beautiful seaside town on the thumb of the hand.

When independence was won the Greek leaders chose Nauplia as the seat of government, and selected a house on the heights above as a palace for the young German whom they made king. But it seems that Nauplia did not please the king as much as it pleases modern visitors, and perhaps the long climb up the 900 steep steps between the town and the palace did not please his officials. At any rate, after a year or two he moved his court and the seat of government to Athens—and so took the center of the new kingdom away from the area where the first great kingdoms of the early Greeks grew up, long before ancient Athens was founded.

The greatest of those early kingdoms was centered on Mycenae, to the north of Nauplia. Its lonely and tremendous ruins look across the rich Argive Plain, now famous for the melons and other produce of its many small fruit farms. And from it the Mycenaean kings ruled much of the Peloponnese. The Mycenaean kings said that they were descended from Pelops, a legendary Greek hero. The name Peloponnese certainly means Island of Pelops, although the area is not quite an island; or rather, it is not quite a *natural* island. Until 1893 it was joined to the mainland by the narrow

The Corinth Canal.

The island of Santorin (in the background) is the top of an old volcano. The smaller island in the foreground rose from the sea in 1928, at about the same time as the city of Corinth was destroyed by an earthquake.

isthmus of Corinth. But in that year the Greeks finished the 11-year task of cutting the Corinth Canal through nearly four miles (six kilometers) of rock, thus turning the Peloponnese into a man-made island, and greatly shortening the sea-journey between eastern Greece and the countries to the west.

People had talked of cutting a canal through the isthmus since

48

the seventh century B.C. One attempt was made about 1,900 years ago. But in those times the need for a canal was not really pressing. Ships were so small that they could be dragged across the isthmus on rollers, while their cargoes were carried across on wagons, pack-animals, and the backs of slaves.

Partly because of this traffic, the city of Corinth (near the southern end of the isthmus) became rich and powerful. St. Paul preached the gospel there. But St. Paul's city was not the Corinth of modern times. Its ruins lie at the foot of a huge fortress-crowned rock called Acrocorinth, and several miles of vineyards separate it from the new Corinth, which is very new indeed. In 1928, the old town was destroyed by one of the earthquakes which come fairly often in Greece, and since then it has been completely rebuilt.

Like ancient Corinth, the new town lives mainly by the trade that results from its position near the isthmus. Land traffic crosses the canal on nearby road and rail bridges, and Corinth is also the nearest port for ships going through the canal. But the main Peloponnesian port for heavier sea-traffic is Patras, about 80 miles (128 kilometers) to the west, at the other end of a narrow coastal plain. Walled in on the south by pine-clad, stony mountains, the plain is a long, leafy belt of citrus groves, olive groves, and vineyards, broken only by fishing villages, a few small towns with whitewashed houses, and holiday camps on the beaches which every year draw thousands of visitors from western Europe. Many of the vineyards grow the small black grapes which when dried become currants, and are an ancient speciality of the north-

Making wine in the Peloponnese. The grapes are pressed twice—first by human feet and then by a screw-press.

ern Peloponnese. In fact, the word *currant* is a shortened mispronunciation of their real name—Corinth raisins.

Some of the currant crop is shipped from the sleepy little port of Aegion, where road, rail, and waterfront run close together at the foot of a hillside town. But the bulk of it goes from the much busier docks of Patras, with large cargoes of other fruit and fruit products. At the Greek end of the main sea-routes between Greece and Italy, Patras is also a very busy passenger port. Its close links with Italy can be seen in the style of its buildings, its arcaded streets, and even the looks and behavior of its people. There is a touch of Italy too in the annual carnival, when the streets are decorated and given over to fancy-dress dances and processions, under showers of confetti and streamers.

With a population of about 150,000, Patras is not large by the standards of more industrialized countries. However, it ranks third in size among the cities of Greece, and is now growing fast as its own industries develop. Greece lacks the coal which has given the factories of some other countries so much of their power. But its many steep mountain-ranges have fast-flowing streams and waterfalls which can be used to generate electricity. Electric power produced in this way is now being used to develop food-processing, weaving, and paper-making industries in Patras and some of the smaller towns in the northern Peloponnese.

Carnival at Patras.

But the Peloponnese is still mainly a farming region. South of Patras, the coastal plain continues and the farmlands widen and flatten as the beautiful but barren limestone mountains fall back. Here, where some of the land lies so low that it can easily be flooded, many of the farmers grow rice, which must spend much of its life in water. And here, by a river among low green hills, lie the white ruins of Olympia, where for nearly 1,200 years crowds from all the Greek states flocked to watch the ancient Olympic Games, while their statesmen talked out plans and problems during the Olympic truce. The grassy spread of ruins is usually a peaceful place, with little to disturb its quiet except the tinkling of a goat bell, a donkey's hoof-plod, and sometimes the scraping of an archaeologist's trowel. But once in every four years it comes alive, and again hears the sound of cheers and running as modern Greek athletes set out on the long relay which carries a flame lit at Olympia to the city of the modern Olympic Games.

Inland from Olympia rise the wild Arcadian mountains, which on their eastern side slope down to a rich central plain with a drier and rather cooler climate than the coast lands. Here, because of the climate, the farm crops are mainly grain, though there are still the grapes and olives that are rarely missing from the Greek countryside. In the surrounding hills, near the town of Tripolis, there are copper mines.

On the road that runs south to the coast lie the ruins of ancient Sparta, whose long-haired soldiers defended the pass of Thermopylae in 480 B.C. and turned the Persian tide at Plataea. But if you are interested in ancient buildings there is little to see

The fortress-castle at Mistra.

at Sparta. The Spartans never bothered to build as strongly as other Greeks did. They said that the "walls" of Sparta were her soldiers. So you would do better to look about three miles (five kilometers) westward at Mistra, a hillside "ghost" town of buildings left over from the days when Greece was ruled by Byzantium, or at the great fortress-castle spread over the ridge above. This frowning fortress-castle seems as though it would be more at home in northwest Europe than in southern Greece. And indeed it would. It was put there by conquering Crusaders, who should have been about their business in the Holy Land.

Of the many ancient buildings in the Peloponnese, the finest is back where we started our journey, on the thumb of the peninsula. If you cross from Nauplia to the outer edge of the thumb, you

53

Modern actors performing in the ancient open-air theater at Epidauros.

come to a place called Epidauros. There, built into a hollow between rocky hills, is a vast theater nearly 2,500 years old and still in use. Like all the theaters of ancient Greece, it was built for performances by daylight. So its 55 curving tiers of solid stone seats lie open to the warm Greek sky. They can hold, without cramming, well over 15,000 people—about ten times as many as a very large modern theater. So carefully are the tiers arranged, that if you stand on the stage and strike one coin with another, a person on the topmost tier can hear the clink.

Epidauros stands high above the coast. Below it is a tiny seaport even older than the theater. From there, by a modern ferryboat, or one of the small Greek sailing ships called *caiques*, we can cross the island-studded Saronic Gulf to Athens and Sterea Hellas.

5

Athens and the Midlands

The northern limits of Greece were once much closer to Athens than they are now. If you imagine a line across the map just north of the long, off-shore island of Euboea, Greece began on the south side. It consisted of the Peloponnese, some islands, and the mainland area south of our line. To distinguish that area from the Peloponnese and the islands, the Greeks called it Sterea Hellas, which means mainland Greece.

Like the rest of the country, Sterea Hellas is largely mountainous. To the west, along the Gulf of Corinth, the mountains are densely massed. Further east, they are broken by hilly plains. Some of these plains are richly fertile. Some, especially in Attica along the far southern coast, are arid because of a very dry climate and the careless cutting of trees in ancient times. And it is on this Attic coast that we begin our visit to Sterea Hellas—at Piraeus, the seaport of Athens.

Piraeus, and Athens too, were no more than villages when the Greeks won their independence from the Turks. Both had lost

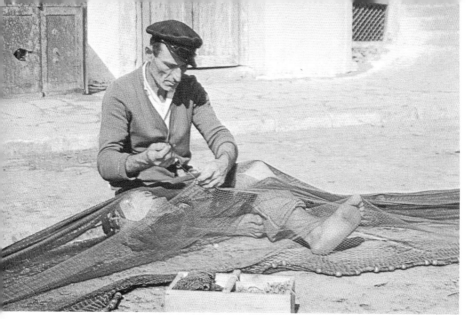

A fisherman mending his nets—feet serve as extra hands.

their ancient importance during the long centuries when Greece was ruled from Byzantium. But they regained it very quickly when Athens became the capital of the new Greek kingdom, and Piraeus is now one of the great ports of the Mediterranean. Piraeus is the home port most of Greece's merchant shipping, as well as the main port of call for foreign vessels, and for many of the small, brightly-colored caiques, some with eyes painted on their bows as in ancient times, which carry people and goods to and from the islands. These slow and sometimes rather rickety caiques and the even smaller fishing boats seem quite at home among the sleek modern passenger liners and giant oil tankers, as do the donkey carts among the huge transport-lorries on the quays; the old winding lanes and crumbling houses among the new broad streets and glassy office buildings; and the fishermen mending their nets among all the bustle of a very up-to-date commercial waterfront. They seem so because Piraeus has managed to make an attractive mixture of old and new—the fishing village of 1832 is still not lost in the 20th century shipping city.

But Piraeus is more than a seaport. Nearby is Hellenikon airport which links Greece with the world's air routes. And, like its Peloponnesian sister Patras, Piraeus is also a rapidly-expanding industrial city. More than half the manufacturing industry of

Piraeus, viewed from the Marina.

Greece is in this part of the country. Piraeus itself produces large quantities of cloth, fertilizers and other chemicals, and tobacco goods. Along the coast to the west are shipyards, that build ships up to 30,000 tons and rebuild much bigger ones. A little further on, the ancient town of Eleusis has become an important industrial center. Once the home of an old Greek religion which drew worshipers from all over the civilized world and had much influence on early Christianity, Eleusis to the modern Greek means oil refineries, weaving factories, steel and cement works. But the small town of Lavrion, southeast of Piraeus, has needed little change to make it fit the modern industrial world. In ancient times, much of the wealth of Athens was drawn from the silver and lead mines of Lavrion. These mines, from their dusty and rather desolate corner of Sterea Hellas, are still contributing to the wealth of Greece.

All these industries and their many workers draw their water supply from the manmade Lake Marathon, away to the northeast. Lake Marathon lies near the battlefield from which the famous Greek athlete took his message to Athens. Among the neighboring mountains is one which, though less than 4,000 feet (6,400 meters) high, appears to be snowcapped all the year round. The mountain is Penteli, and the "snow fields" are really the gleaming white marble quarries, still being worked, from which the material of the many magnificent buildings of ancient Athens was taken.

If you have a picture of Athens in your mind, it will almost certainly include one of those buildings—the breathtakingly beautiful Parthenon temple, glowing golden on the great, steep, flat-topped rock called the Acropolis. Indeed, your only mental picture of the city may be of the Parthenon and the Acropolis, because for people who have not seen Athens it is often only a city of ruins, an aged and sleepy city living on what is left of the art and architecture which startled the ancient world and still influences the modern. But when they visit Athens those people find very quickly that they must revise their picture.

There certainly are old buildings and the ruins of old buildings, many of them made of that white Pentelic marble which turns

Quarrying marble blocks on Mount Penteli. The marble of the Parthenon came from here.

The Parthenon is not the only temple on the Acropolis. This is part of the Erectheion, a smaller temple nearby. The marble maidens (Caryatids) support a roof weighing more than two tons (over 2,000 kilograms).

golden as it ages. There are also many museums full of the art and craft work that decorated the buildings, and of the objects, usually well-made and good to look at, which the people of the time used in their daily lives. But for all its ancient background Athens is a modern city, modern in its buildings, modern in its industries and transportation, and modern in the activities of its 3,500,000

60

people, who are moving right into the 21st century and very much awake—except between lunchtime and late afternoon, when the sun beating in from the south makes everyone drowsy, and the city closes down for siesta.

Unlike Piraeus, Athens has not mixed the old with the new very much. The old Athens stops short at the maze of narrow streets and ruins and rather shabby houses around the foot of the Acropolis, and from there the modern city spreads out past Mount Lycabettos, a green cone-shaped hill crowned by a white chapel, which is as much a landmark to the east as the Acropolis is to the south. Much rebuilt and extended in recent years, the modern city was planned and laid out only a little more than 100 years ago, with broad, straight streets and many squares and gardens.

The chapel of St. George on the summit of Mount Lycabettos. The lower slopes are a modern residential area.

The squares and gardens are very popular among Athenians, who like to spend most of their spare time in public places, always with brightly polished shoes—there are more shoeshine boys in the streets of Athens than in any other city of the world—and often carrying a flower or clicking a string of yellow beads. The beads, called *komboloia* in Greek and worry beads in English, are sometimes thought by visitors to be used in praying, like the rosary beads of Roman Catholics. But they are not. Greeks carry them and click them simply because they like to have something to do with their hands.

Athenians also like to stay out late at night. After all, they have had that long rest through the heat of the afternoon, so why should they want to go to bed early? And, because they stay out late, shops and cafés stay open much later than they usually do in the cities of cooler countries; so do the many little pavement kiosks lining the streets and squares. These seem to sell anything small enough to fit behind their counters, and some of them are ready to sell it from one sunset to the next. There are also many sellers from wheelbarrows, baskets, and trays and from their own shoulders—sellers who offer all the produce of Greece from bananas to pistachio nuts, from delicious chewy slabs of seed held together with honey to the soft yellow bath sponges that divers bring up from the waters of the Aegean and Mediterranean seas.

Naturally enough, they all shout their wares. But perhaps because they are Greeks they do it even more noisily than the street-vendors of other countries. The traffic is noisy, too. Greek drivers love their horns, and they seem to delight in shouted argument with other drivers as they struggle for a place in the dense mass of traffic. And from pedestrian crowds and café-sitters there is always a surge of talk, and the clicking of worry beads. Even the evzones (the white-kilted soldiers sometimes seen on guard duty) manage to make more noise with their soft pompommed slippers than a grenadier does with his boots. So the visitor who goes to Athens with only a picture of the ancient city in his mind is much more likely to leave it with the loud and lively echoes of the modern city in his ears.

North and west of Athens, the dry Attic plain is shut in by mountains. Beyond them lies the rest of Sterea Hellas, another area of hilly plains running east to the Aegean Sea and the island of Euboea (Evia). Euboea, over 100 miles (160 kilometers) long, counts as part of Sterea Hellas because it lies so close to the mainland. At one point they are joined by a swing bridge no longer than a soccer field; and if you look down from the bridge you can see something that is very rare round the Mediterranean coastline. Normally, the Mediterranean Sea has no real tide, or so little tide that it is impossible to tell the difference between high and low. But in the strait between Euboea and the mainland a swiftly flowing current changes direction as often as six times a day; and at every change the water rises or falls sharply, like the ebb and flow of a real tide.

There is an old saying that poverty and Greece are sisters, and nowhere is that more obvious than on Euboea. In parts of the south, it is barely possible for farmers to scratch a living from the rocky soil; and though the north is more fertile, the small size of

Typical Greek food shops in a city market.

the farms and the lack of roads leading to markets have kept the farmers almost as poor as their southern neighbors. However, many Euboeans have now found work in new manufacturing industries at the old town of Chalcis near the end of the bridge from the mainland. In the north, a welfare organization (with support from British people) has helped to improve both farms and standards of living.

Back on the mainland, the farms are much more productive. In fact, it was this region which grew most of the wheat used in ancient Athens, and it still provides much for the modern city. It also supplies some of the raw cotton for the spinning and weaving industries of Athens and Piraeus, and it does so from an area

A popular holiday place on the Attic coast.

which was once the vast, shallow Lake Copais. Around the year 1900, some British businessmen leased the lake from the Greek government, drained it, and for many years ran it as one big farm. Then it passed back to the government. They divided it into many small farms and gave them to Greeks who wanted to be farmers but could find no land. The farms are run cooperatively, with the farmers sharing work, equipment, and profits. Though the profits are not large by the standards of some other countries, this is now one of the more prosperous small-farming areas of Greece.

Cotton pickers on a farm in the Copais area.

Off the western limits of the plain rises the great mountain mass of Parnassos, where mist, storm, and cloud movement make constant and sometimes awe-inspiring changes in the clear Greek light. Here, looking down from the southern slopes over a grey sea of olive trees to the real sea, stand the ruins of Delphi, the main sanctuary of the god Apollo. Delphi was more than a temple, more than a center of the old Greek religions. Like Olympia, it was a neutral ground where the leaders of the Greek city-states came to talk over disputes and alliances, and where a regular festival, with music, poetry and drama as well as athletic games, was held. But now we remember it chiefly as a seat of the Delphic oracle—a priestess through whom Apollo was supposed to answer when a worshiper asked for advice. History has shown that some of the answers were remarkably accurate. But more often than not the answer had more than one meaning, so that the oracle could be right whatever happened. For instance, when a king once asked if he should make war on a neighbor, the oracle said: "Do so and you will destroy a mighty kingdom." The inquirer did so— but the kingdom destroyed was his own.

Westward from Delphi, at the mouth of the Corinthian Gulf, the mountains slope down to a flat land of marshes and lagoons around the fishing town of Missolonghi. Missolonghi is famous for a long and terrible siege by the Turks during the war of independence. And in the town square there is a memorial to the British poet Byron, a philhellene who thought of Greece as his true home, and who died while helping the Greeks to withstand the siege.

The ruins of Delphi cover a vast area. These temples are only a small part of them.

Nearby the visitor can board a bus that will almost certainly be crammed with chickens, goats, bicycles, and packages of all kinds, as well as people, and start a sometimes hair-raising drive over the mountain roads into northern Greece.

6

Up North

The northwestern corner of Greece is called Epirus. A stark, cool, ruggedly mountainous region, it has sometimes been likened to the highlands of Scotland—and not only because its national costume is the kilt worn by the evzone guard regiment. It is also like the highlands of Scotland because it lay isolated and preserving an old way of life behind a massive mountain barrier through the long centuries when travel was difficult; and because its people, hardy and rather warlike but hospitable shepherd-farmers, are intensely proud and independent. Their fierce independence is a byword even among their independence-minded fellow-Greeks. Before the rest of Greece began its struggle for freedom, they had tried to make Epirus an independent state—in alliance with their Turkish governor.

The governor, Ali Pasha, wanted to be an independent ruler, and with the help of his Greek subjects he managed to keep Epirus free of Turkish interference for more than 30 years. In return for their help, the Greeks of Epirus were given freedom and opportunities that they had not known for centuries. And—

because Ali saw himself as a future ruler of the whole country—he encouraged them and paid them to stir up rebellion among their fellow-Greeks. As you know, the rebellion succeeded in the regions further south. But the Greeks could not hold Epirus. Ali's independent state was crushed. And Epirus remained under Turkish rule until 1913.

Because the Turks left so recently, there is still very much that is Turkish about Jannina, the main town of the region and Ali Pasha's old capital. It can be seen in the furnishings and decoration of the houses, in the food and the habits and some of the clothes of the people, in the lively bazaar which sells the work of the city's highly-skilled silversmiths and other craftsmen, and most noticeably of all in the Muslim minarets and the storks which are encouraged to nest on the rooftops. Among its population there are many non-Greeks, including Jews who, like the

Mosques and minarets from the centuries of Turkish rule at lakeside Jannina.

Goats coming home down a mountain road.

Jews of the Thessaloniki area, lived here comfortably and undisturbed until the Germans took the city in the Second World War.

Though Epirus is mainly a highland country, Jannina is a lowland city. It lies ringed by mountains on a broad, flat agricultural plain, and is strikingly placed on a promontory which juts into a deep, dark lake, rich in fish and eels.

Outside Jannina, most Epirote people are still shepherd-farmers. Some of them are partly nomadic, camping with their belled sheep and goats high on the mountainsides during the summer, and bringing them home to the valleys for the long, severe and often stormy winter. This method of pastoral farming is called transhumance, and is also practised by the Vlachs, many of whom live in

72

and around the high-perched, stone-built town of Metsovo and in the mountains further east.

The road running eastward from Metsovo winds and climbs through country that looks like a warmer Switzerland. In one of the valleys, almost midway between the west and the east coasts, there is a village of pink, blue, and white houses called Kalambaka. Kalambaka is known for its sawmills, and if seen by itself it would seem much like any other village among the green pastures and fruit farms below these heavily wooded mountains. But it cannot be seen by itself. Behind it rises a serried mass of

Milled timber from the mountains of northern Greece awaiting export.

A farmer of Metsovo. Notice his worry-beads and the stone houses in the background.

huge natural monoliths—free-standing stones broader and taller than skyscrapers.

If you are energetic enough you can climb some of them, by the thousands of steps that take you to the Meteora monasteries. Some people explain the name Meteora by saying that long ago some meteors fell on the district and caused the rocks. But that is wrong. In the Greek language, the word *meteora* has several meanings. One of them is "hanging in mid-air." Once you have toiled to a rock-top you can see which meaning was in the minds of the men who named the monasteries. You really feel that the building is hung in mid-air—and likely to drop at any moment. But none of the 24 has plummeted down in the 600 years since the first was built. The Orthodox monks and laymen who came to the Meteora to escape from religious wars and persecutions could have found no safer refuge. Until recently, there were not even steps to take you to the rock-tops. You had to be hauled up in a basket on the end of a rope. Nowadays, some of the monasteries

One of the Meteora monasteries.

are empty, and others have fallen into ruin. But several are still very much occupied by busy and kindly monks who are glad to welcome you if you care to test your leg muscles with the climb.

When you have reached the Meteora you are out of Epirus and into Thessaly, a land of vast plains running northward to Mount Olympus. Like the Lake Copais area in Sterea Hellas, the plains of Thessaly were once under water. But here the drainage was not the work of man. In prehistoric times, the mountains which surround Thessaly were the shores of an inland sea. Later, natural

Spinning thread by hand, a much older craft than wheel-spinning.

upheavals turned the sea into freshwater lakes. And still later upheavals drained the lakes to leave rich lowlands which now supply Greece with great quantities of wheat, maize (Indian corn), and cotton.

In ancient times, Thessaly was famous for its horses; and very fine horses are still bred on its upland pastures. So too are cattle and sheep, many of the sheep-flocks belonging to the picturesque and nomadic Vlachs. Because the area is almost wholly agricultural, towns are few and small, and the townsfolk live mainly by trading with farmers and by marketing and moving their products. But light manufacturing industries are developing in the road and railway junction of Larissa, and in the busy little seaport of Volos—very new-looking because it was rebuilt after being seriously damaged by an earthquake in 1955. There is also a very small town whose only product would delight people anywhere but is, alas, usually to be had only in Greece. This town is Pharsala, the site of a famous battle in Roman times and now famous because it makes *halvas*—a very sticky nougat, said to be the best in Greece.

North, beyond Mount Olympus, lie Macedonia and Thrace, the great tobacco-growing provinces, and Thessaloniki the capital of Macedonia. Thessaloniki, is the second largest city of Greece in population. The site of a university and an important international trade fair, it is a new city framed by an old one, as the entire city center has been rebuilt since a disastrous fire during the First World War and serious air-raid damage in the Second World War. The new buildings stand on a level area near the waterfront.

New buildings on the waterfront at Thessaloniki. Many of the caiques that carry passengers and cargo to the Aegean Islands sail from here.

Behind them and on either side are the old ones, many Turkish and some Byzantine. They rise up the surrounding slopes and look out to a harbor that is second only to Piraeus in the volume and variety of its shipping.

But it is not the great mass of merchant shipping that draws the eye in a walk along Thessaloniki's broad and tree-lined waterfront. Much more attractive are the *gri-gri* boats, called *ducks* by the local children. These are brightly painted fishing boats which go out in groups, a large one ahead, five or six small ones strung behind, like a duck leading her ducklings. The gri-gri fishermen are often out at night, with lamps on the bows of the smaller boats to attract the fish. If you look down from the old city then, the harbor seems like a darkened stage, and the gri-gri boats a ballet of dancing lights.

North of Thessaloniki, and eastward to the furthest extent of Thrace, spread the farmlands which, with Thessaly's, grow the greater part of the agricultural produce of Greece. From this region too come the majority of the country's minerals. These include asbestos, bauxite, lead, uranium, and also lignite, a kind of coal which in the north is used as an alternative to water for

At these modern works, aluminum is extracted from bauxite mined in the mountains.

Olive groves with old gnarled trees like these are a familiar sight throughout Greece.

driving electricity generators. These, and other minerals, have helped Greece to develop important new export and manufacturing industries in recent years.

7

The Islands

Blue and white are the colors of the Greek flag, and they are also the colors of the Greek islands. There are other colors as well, of

Blue and white on the island of Hydra, off the Peloponnese.

A typical island church. This one is on Sifnos in the Cyclades.

course—the many colors of growing things where the islands are fertile, and of rock where they are not. But blue and white are the colors that you remember—blue sea, white houses, blue sky. Not that the seas are always blue. In those Persian wars of long ago, the Greeks were greatly helped by storms which wrecked many of the enemy ships. And storms of the same kind often darken the sky and sea today and endanger caiques and fishing boats, especially around the islands in the Aegean Sea. Nor are there always houses. Of the 1,425 islands lying off the Greek mainland, only about 160 are inhabited, and some of those have so few people

82

that their houses are barely noticeable. But those things are easily forgotten. It is the inhabited islands and the bright calm days that force themselves upon visitors, filling their minds with sweeps of sparkling blue and blocks of dazzling white.

The islands make up one fifth of the total area of Greece. Most are in the Aegean Sea or the approaches to the Aegean, and most lie in groups, which sometimes spread so far that on a small map it is hard to decide whether a particular island belongs to one group or another, or even to any group. They are naturally rugged, but wind and storm have made many of them more so. Some are so infertile that little can be grown there except in tubs and pots. On these islands the people live mainly by fishing and handicrafts, and the young men, brought up to be as much at home on the sea as on the land, provide a steady supply of seamen for the huge Greek merchant navy.

Sailing south from Thessaloniki the nearest islands are a group called the Sporades. The name means "scattered." And as these scattered islands have a greater depth of good soil and a milder climate than most, some are well wooded and produce a great deal of fruit. One, Skopelos, is especially noted for its purple plums, most of which are dried first in the sun and then in the ovens, and exported as prunes. The most easterly island of the group, Skyros, also has a speciality, this time a handicraft. If you visit a Greek home you may well be invited to sit on a low, finely-carved wooden chair; and this will almost certainly have come from Skyros, or have been made to a Skyros pattern. Other handicrafts of this partly barren island are pottery, embroidery, and weaving. Skyros is also a favorite vacation island for Greeks from the mainland, and it interests British visitors because the poet Rupert Brooke is buried here. He had died onboard ship (not far from Skyros) while serving as a naval officer in the First World War.

East and south of Skyros are some ungrouped islands which include the mountainous Chios, legendary birthplace of the Greek poet Homer, whose poems have given us the stories of the siege of Troy and of the adventurous journeys of Odysseus. It is also the home of what was probably the first chewing gum—a scented substance secreted from trees which are cultivated on the island. Called *mastic*, it may be asked for in Greek cafés, where you will be served a spoonful of it submerged in a glass of water. You may drink the scented water and then chew the gum, or sip and chew by turns as you wish.

South of the ungrouped islands begin the Dodecanese, also called the Southern Sporades. Dodecanese means "12 islands," but there are 14 in the group besides the small uninhabited ones. Strung out in a slightly curving line around the southwest corner of Turkey, they seem naturally part of Turkey rather than of Greece, but their people are mainly Greek, descendants of Greek settlers who came across the Aegean in ancient times. However, they have only recently become part of modern Greece. They were held by the Turks until 1912 and then taken over by the Italians, who did not return them to Greece until 1948.

The largest of the Dodecanese is Rhodes, mountainous but richly fertile as can be guessed from its name, which means "place of roses." Roses are still cultivated there, and so too are other

Island houses are built along narrow lanes, these are on Skyros.

flowers, citrus fruits, grapes, tobacco, and olives. Unlike most other Greek islands, Rhodes is large enough to have room for wild animals. Deer, hares and foxes are all plentiful in the mountains. In the island capital, also called Rhodes, the West European look of many of the old buildings reminds the visitor that for 200 years Rhodes was the headquarters of the Knights of St. John of Jerusalem, the famous order of French, British, Italian, Spanish, and German Crusaders who specialized in medical treatment as well as in trying to take the Holy Land from the Turks. (Their name is preserved by the St. John Ambulance Association.) Also on the island of Rhodes is the ancient harbor of Lindos, where St. Paul landed on one of his missionary journeys.

Other Dodecanese of special interest are Patmos, Cos, and Calymnos. It was during a long exile on the monastery island of Patmos, part of the rocky crater of a submerged volcano, that St. John wrote the New Testament book of *Revelation.* On Cos at the time of the Golden Age lived Hippocrates, the great medical scientist of ancient Greece. Later doctors came to regard him as the "father of medicine." All doctors are expected to follow a code of professional behavior which he laid down; some take what is called the "Hippocratic Oath." Coming back to the present, on red-cliffed Calymnos live many of the sponge-divers whose dangerous work supplies the sponges sold in the markets of Athens and very widely exported. The men of the island are nearly all sponge-divers, and, as most of them work off the African coast, Calymnos becomes an island of women and children during the summer diving season.

Sponge graders at work. They measure the sponges by passing them through holes of different sizes.

Their houses are often painted blue instead of the usual white, a habit which goes back to the time when they were under foreign rule. Then, every second house was painted blue, so that the blue and white rows should match the Greek flag and show the rulers that they were not welcome.

Westward of the Dodecanese and coming close to the mainland are the Cyclades. In the word bicycle, the "*cycle*" part comes from a Greek word meaning a ring and thus a wheel, so you could guess that the Cyclades form a ring. They form it around the small island of Delos, in ancient times a very rich trading center and a sanctuary of the god Apollo even more important than Delphi on the mainland. It is now in ruins, and inhabited only when caiques from the neighboring island of Mykonos bring sheep across to graze. Without Delos, the sheep might well go hungry, as Mykonos, like most of the Cyclades, is too barren and short of water to grow good grass or farm crops. Nearby is Siros, unusual as the only Aegean island with a heavy industry. Its very modern shipyard builds ships of up to 30,000 tons, and thus keeps happily at home many islanders who would otherwise have to seek work on the mainland or in foreign countries. Perhaps more interesting, though less important to Greece, is the second industry of Siros. It makes Turkish delight, called *loukoumia* in Greek, a nougat which rivals that of Pharsala in Thessaly.

Southward from the Cyclades lies Crete, the largest and most prosperous of the Greek islands, and the island where Theseus established the power of ancient Greece by finding his way

Apollo's sanctuary on Delos was guarded by these sculptured lions.

This cup is about 3,500 years old. It came from Mycenae in the Peloponnese, but the bull design is Cretan.

through the maze to kill the Minotaur. Of course, we need not believe that there really was a Minotaur. But the bull was a sacred animal to the ancient Cretans. Their kings appear to have worn a bull-mask at religious ceremonies. And the vast ruins of their palace at Knossos near modern Herakleion show that it would have been very difficult for a stranger to find his way about. So we can believe that some ancient Greek—perhaps his name really was Theseus and perhaps he had an army behind him—managed to get through the maze of corridors to the bull-masked king and kill him.

As for the island itself, it has a high mountain backbone broken by fertile but sometimes dry valleys and plateaux, and the fact

An old man of Crete, with traditional boots, breeches, and dagger.

that it has only two large towns in an area of over 3,000 square miles (8,000 square kilometers) shows that most of its 500,000 people must be farmers. Like the mountain farmers of Epirus on the mainland, they are proud, brave, and fiercely independent, as German invaders found out in the Second World War. They are also very much inclined to keep to old ways, in both their work and their behavior. Many of the men still wear the traditional costume of black breeches and high boots, with a scarlet-lined cloak over a blue jacket, and a silver-sheathed dagger at the waist. The dagger is not for decoration. To strangers, Cretans are friendly and, if anything, more hospitable than the mainland Greeks. But among themselves their hot tempers often lead to feuds and bloodshed.

To the north of Crete and on the west side of the mainland are the seven Ionian islands and their many neighboring islets, different from the islands of the Aegean both in nature and in what man has done to them. Nature has given them such rich vegetation that they look almost tropical. Man has developed them in such a way that they look more Italian than Greek—or rather, Italian with a touch of British. The Italian look, and the Italian blood in their people, comes from their having been held by the Italian city of Venice for 600 years. The British influence came in the 19th century, when they were part of the British Empire until Britain handed them back to Greece in 1864.

In Homer's story-poem these were the islands of the wandering Odysseus who, when at home, was the king of Ithaca. The royal family of modern Greece also had a home in the islands, on Corfu. It is the birthplace of Britain's Duke of Edinburgh, who was born Prince Philip of Greece.

One of the group, Leukas, is not really an island. Originally joined to the mainland, it became an island when a canal was cut through the narrow isthmus, and from there we can make the very short journey back to Sterea Hellas and take a closer look at the lives of Greek people.

8

Home, Holidays, and School

Spartans aside, the ancient Greeks put more craftsmanship, artistry, and loving interest into the construction and decoration of their public buildings than any other people before or after them. But their houses were very simple, so simple that visitors often asked themselves how a free people who had planned and built such a wonder as the Parthenon could be content to live below it in what were little more than sparsely-furnished and undecorated huts. Even the very rich, whose money paid for much of the magnificent public buildings, had modest tastes in the size and furnishing of their own homes. They needed no more because they liked to spend so much of their time in public places that home was mainly a place for sleeping. Though most modern Greeks live more comfortably than their Parthenon-building ancestors, their attitude is much the same.

Partly because of this, and partly because so many modern Greeks earn very little money, their homes are often small, simply furnished, and without much of the equipment which people in some other countries believe to be necessary. This is especially true in the country districts and on the islands, where a family home is sometimes a two-roomed cottage, usually one room up and one room down with an outside staircase. The downstairs room is often used as a shelter for animals and for storage, and the family lives in the upstairs room, with beds and a few pieces of simple furniture along the walls. Some of the family's food is cooked outside the cottage, in an oven made of hardened mud. An open indoor fireplace serves for the rest. Pots hang over the fire from iron tripods—three-legged stands such as are often used for camp cooking.

Country and island families with more money to spare have larger houses that allow more privacy, but they remain fairly sim-

Flat roofs on an Aegean island.

ple. Built of stone and color-washed, they usually keep to outside staircases and sometimes to outside ovens, and a good many have neither bathrooms nor inside sanitation. In many places there is no piped water. Drinking and cooking water must be carried from the village well, and sometimes laundry water too. But in places near running streams the washing is often taken to the stream, perhaps by donkey if there is a lot of it, and done there. Some places still lack electricity, too, and houses are lit by oil or candles.

Mainland people prefer pitched roofs, usually covered with brownish-red tiles, while islanders like their roofs flat, or sometimes slightly domed. But island or mainland, town or country, there are few Greek houses that do not have a trellised grapevine, for shady outdoor living as much as for the fruit. There are also very few houses without a religious picture, called an ikon, on a living room wall, often with a little oil-lamp or candle burning below it. You often see ikons outside the home, too. Churches set them up by roadsides and in other public places. They hang in shops and offices. Taxi and bus drivers like to fix them in their vehicles, and they are often carried on fishing boats and farm-carts.

There are so many ikons about because the Greeks as a whole are a very religious people, and strongly attached to their Orthodox church though kindly tolerant of other faiths, Christian and non-Christian. Because of this, the two great festivals of the Christian year, Easter and Christmas, are celebrated more noticeably and with greater public feeling than they are in many other Christian countries. Easter is the more important, and is a time

94

Some of the many shapes in which Greeks make *koulouria*, their traditional Easter biscuits.

first of fasting and magnificent but mournful processions, and then of joyous bell-ringing, fireworks, music and noisy feasting on special food—dyed eggs, biscuits cut into a vast variety of shapes, and an Easter lamb. Among the very poor people, the Easter lamb may be the only red meat of the year. But they are always ready to bring in a passing stranger and offer him a share.

St. Nicholas, the original of Santa Claus, was a Greek but has no part in the Greek Christmas. However, creatures very like his opposite are supposed to appear on Christmas Eve and remain over the 12 days of Christmas. These are a kind of goblin called *Kallikantzari*, and though nobody has ever seen one they are believed to get up to all kinds of mischief. Perhaps they are just a good opportunity for children at home over the holiday to put the blame on someone else. Children are given sweets and nuts at Christmas, but no other presents. For those, they have to wait for New Year's Day, or St. Basil's Day as they more often call it.

Christmas Day itself is a religious occasion rather than a day of merriment, but a good deal of merriment follows it, ending with a noisy carnival on Epiphany, the last of the 12 days. There are many other holidays and festivals in the Greek calendar, mainly on saints's days. Each village has a special saint and takes time off to celebrate his day, usually with feasting, processions, music and dancing, and often in very colorful traditional clothing. Sometimes there is also a traveling shadow play, always about the comic adventures of a character called *Karaghiosis*.

For many Greek country people, these festivals are the main form of entertainment apart from talking, which could almost be called the national hobby, and listening to radio and television programs. Nearly every dwelling has a radio of some kind, but many still do not have a television, and most villages are too small to have a movie theater. But the Greeks are very good at entertaining themselves, and boredom is a very rare complaint among them.

At any festival, or in any village at ordinary times, you are sure to meet at least one Greek who dresses a little differently from the rest, and perhaps looks a little more prosperous. If he hears you speaking English, he will greet you heartily and tell you that he has spent much of his life in America, or Britain, or Australia, or some other part of the English-speaking world—and he will also tell you very politely that although he enjoyed himself abroad, he was glad when he had saved enough money to go back to Greece. Many Greek emigrants are like that. Thousands of them go abroad to work. Very few of them go abroad to settle. For all the advantages of New York or Sydney or London, most Greeks would rather live at home. And if they can save enough money, they go back.

Some of them will have left Greece when they were quite young, and perhaps without much schooling. Until fairly recently, Greek governments spent very little money on education. In the 1950s, more than half the people could neither read nor write; even in the 1960s, most children left school at the age of 12, or even earlier. However, there have been great improvements since then. Education is now free and compulsory for all children between the ages of six and 15. It is also free for children over 15, but many children who are over 15 cannot benefit from it because their homes are too far from towns with suitable schools.

In some of the larger towns, the primary schools have roomy, pleasant buildings. But in villages the school buildings are often small, cramped and very poorly equipped, and sometimes have only one teacher. Not many schools have gym periods or games

Entertainment on a caique in the Dodecanese. The man wearing a hat is playing a small bagpipe. His friend's instrument is a *lyra*.

arranged by the teachers, nor are team games much played after school. But most schools end the term or the school year with athletic contests, and these keep to the tradition of the ancient Greek games by mixing music and dancing with the other events on the program.

Saturday is a school day in Greece, but every school day is shorter than it is in countries where schools have a five-day week. Lessons end at lunchtime, but in the country children who live a long way from school have their meal, often cooked over an open fire in the school grounds, before they go home. Even in the towns, for most children the midday meal will consist of local produce—fresh fruit and vegetables in season, dried fruit, bread from locally ground flour, and with olive oil instead of butter, cheese from the milk of local goats, and perhaps fish if they live by the sea. And, of course, there will be water to drink. The Greeks are great drinkers of water. They always take a glass of water with a cup of coffee; to tea drinkers, which they are not, they sometimes serve a glass of water with a cup of tea.

There may also be a little wine with the meal, but though Greece is a wine-producing country most Greeks drink only in moderate quantities. When they do drink wine, it is often flavored with a special resin taken from a tree called the Aleppo pine which grows in the forest areas. This resin is also used in chemical industries.

Among people who can afford meat, favorite dishes are meatballs with various sauces, and mincemeat mixed with rice and herbs and rolled up in vine-leaves. Greeks rarely have puddings, but they do like sweet things, which are often made with honey instead of sugar, and thick with nuts or seeds. Even some of the milder cheeses, and sheep's milk yogurt, are eaten with honey.

With the smallest quantity of food that you take with another person, it is good manners in Greece to raise your glass of water (there is sure to be a glass of water) and say "*steen hee-án sass.*" This means roughly what we mean when we say "Good health." So let us say "*Steen hee-án sass*" to the Greeks in the hope that they will soon settle their problems and take as great a part in shaping the civilization of the future as their ancestors took in shaping our own.

GLOSSARY

acropolis Defensible high ground around which the Greeks built their cities

caiques Light boat

city-state Division of ancient Greece consisting of one city and the countryside around it

gri-gri boats Brightly painted fishing boats that travel in groups with one large one in the lead and four or five smaller ones following, like a duck leading ducklings.

halvas A very sticky nougat candy made only in Greece

ikon Religious picture painted on a small piece of wood usually hung on walls in homes and churches in the eastern Catholic religions

isthmus Narrow strip of land connecting two larger land areas

komboloia Worry beads carried by some Greeks that they rub to keep their hands busy

logic The art of thinking clearly, of finding our way to the truth by the use of reason

monoliths A single free-standing large stone, usually very tall

Parthenon A famous Doric temple built on the acropolis of Athens in the fifth century B.C.

philhellenc Someone who admires or loves Greece and things that are Greek

INDEX